AMAZING SECRET OF THE AMERICAN'S STRONG ECONOMY:

Unravelling the Foundations Of Prosperity

By

John A. Smith

1

TABLE OF CONTENTS

DISCLAIMER

DESCRIPTION

"The Amazing Secret of America's Strong Economy: Unravelling the Foundations of Prosperity", is an in-depth and comprehensive analysis of the factors that shape America's strong economic landscape. In this groundbreaking book, **author John A. Smith** delves into a complex web of economic, social, and political factors that contribute to a country's sustainable financial growth, prosperity and well-being, and global competitiveness.

This eye-opening journey into the unique economic power of the United States sheds light on the intricacies of trade policies, taxes and fiscal responsibility.

Smith sees the role of innovation, entrepreneurship and a diverse workforce as key factors in creating economic opportunity and driving growth.

The book also explores the importance of social mobility, the influence of the Federal Reserve, and the nation's ability to adapt and overcome challenges in times of crisis.

Smith sheds light on the paradox of American wealth due to the contribution of the diaspora to the strength of the financial industry and the exceptional nature of the nation in a global context.

Through meticulous research, compelling case studies, and gripping anecdotes, The Powerful Secrets of America's Strong Economy gives readers an unparalleled understanding of the pillars that underpin the thriving United States economy.

This book is aimed at economists, historians, policymakers, business professionals, and general readers seeking to unravel the intricate circumstances that drive business success.

Readers will be drawn into an exciting adventure as they discover the extraordinary interplay of elements in the annals of economic history that make America's strong economy a source of power, truly an indispensable resource.

INTRODUCTION

The United States is the largest economy in the world by gross domestic product (GDP). The country has a vibrant and resilient economy that inspires fascination and admiration around the world. The secret to this economic success may seem elusive, but this book begins by exploring the many factors that contribute to the strength of the American economy. Dive into the key drivers of US prosperity and find out how we can learn from the US experience.

CHAPTER 1

A Brief History of the American Economy

The American economy has undergone many changes since its founding. This brief history examines some of its key moments and stages of development. **1. Colonial Period (1607–1775):** The colonies had a predominantly agricultural economy, with agriculture and cattle ranching as the backbone of economic activity.

Tobacco in particular plays an important role in South America. Additionally, the North is engaged in modest commercial and industrial activity, setting the stage for future growth.

2. First Republic (1776-1820): During the Revolutionary War, international trade was disrupted, leading to a focus on self-reliance and the use of American resources. However, Alexander Hamilton's initiatives, such as the creation of the First Bank of the United States, laid a solid economic foundation.

The famous cotton separator revolutionized the textile industry and paved the way for industrialization, and the Louisiana Purchase of 1803 aided westward expansion.

3. Industrial Revolution (1820-1870): The United States began to industrialize during this period, with advances in transportation (canals, steamships, and railroads) and manufacturing,

Leading to a significant increase in energy production. The South is still predominantly agricultural and focuses on cotton production.

The wave of European immigration provided the labour force for the growth of urban centres.

4. After the Civil War to the end of the 19th century: this so-called "Golden Age" saw the emergence of powerful tycoons such as Rockefeller, Vanderbilt and Carnegie, who founded imperial corporations, national institutions and large organizations, often through monopolies.

The economy also experienced several recessions and financial crises during this period.

However, the advent of the gold standard and the rise of the stock market have increased the desire to expand.

5. Progressive Era (1890-1920) discourse attempted to hide the inequality and political corruption fuelled by rapid industrialization. Labour movements and social reforms have been significant, leading to workers' rights and better working conditions. Antitrust laws and financial regulations also emerged during this period.

6. 1920s Boom: The 1920s prosperity, characterized by rapid economic growth, consumerism, and innovative industries like automobiles and radios, was what couldn't. Luck leads to greed and abundance. It is an abrupt stop.

7. The New Deal (1933-1938): President Franklin D. Roosevelt enacted many fiscal policies and reforms to combat the deep economic crisis of the 1930s. Unemployment insurance, minimum wages, and public works were instituted to help stabilize the country.

8. Post WWII to 1960s: The US economy flourished after WWII as global demand for American goods increased.

The United States has experienced a period of economic prosperity, the growth of a consumer culture and the promotion of civil rights has marked this period.

9. 1970s and 1980s: During the energy crisis, high inflation and economic stagnation, US production declined while global competition increased. The Reagan era brought deregulation, tax cuts, and economic growth to the service sector.

10 1990s-present: The tech boom of the 1990s solidified the United States' leadership in innovation and the digital economy. Globalization and trade deals are being redefined as redundant global trade relations.

The 2001 and 2008 recessions led to regulatory measures to stabilize the economy.

In modern America, technological innovations continue to drive economic growth, with a growing emphasis on services, E-commerce and the informal economy.

The Early Foundations: From Colonial Times to the Civil War: America's Early Formation Between Colonialism and the Civil War covers many important historical events and figures who helped shape America's future.

The following is a summary of some of the major events and circumstance that took place from the Colonial Period to the Civil War:

1. Colonial Period (1607-1763) Jamestown Settlement (1607): Jamestown, Virginia today is the area the first successful colonization area British colonists settled in North America.

Founded by the Virginia Company, a group of British investors, the settlement marked Britain's first major foothold on the continent.

The Pilgrims and Plymouth Colony (1620) - A group of religious dissenters known as the Pilgrims came to North America aboard the Mayflower and settled at Plymouth Rock in present-day Massachusetts. They established Plymouth Colony, which formed the basis for later colonies in New England.

Great Migration (1620-1640): A significant number of English settlers migrated to the New World in search of religious freedom and economic opportunity.

They established several colonies, mainly in eastern North America.

Relations with Native Americans: The arrival of Europeans in the Americas led to many conflicts and trade relations with Native Americans. European settlers often relied on local knowledge and resources, but their search for land and resources eventually led to stress, disease, and violence.

2. Revolutionary period (1763-1783) Tension between Britain and the colonies (1763–1775): The British government imposed new taxes and laws on the American colonies such as the Stamp Act (1765) and the Tea Act (1773).

These actions angered the colonists, who protested and took actions such as the Boston Tea Party (1773).

American Revolutionary War (1775-1783): Tensions eventually led to a series of conflicts culminating in the American Revolutionary War of 1775.

Under the leadership of leaders such as George Washington, military Mainland China was formed to fight the British.

Declaration of Independence (1776): Thomas Jefferson and the other Founding Fathers wrote this document declaring the colony's decision to secede from Great Britain.

Treaty of Paris (1783): The American Revolutionary War officially ended with the Treaty of Paris, in which Great Britain recognized the independence of the United States and agreed to a series of territorial agreements

3. First Republic (1783-1820) Establishment of the United States Constitution (1787): The United States Constitution, still the basic law of the nation, was signed by 39 delegates to the Constituent Assembly and created a new framework for federal government. **Bill of Rights (1791):** Ratified the first ten amendments to the United States Constitution to guarantee individual freedoms and protections.

Presidency of George Washington (1789-1797):

Washington's presidency set important precedents, such as the two-term limit and the president's role as national leader. Louisiana Purchase (1803): President Thomas Jefferson's purchase of most of France doubled the size of the United States and facilitated westward expansion.

Four Pre-war Missouri Compromise (1820-1860) (1820):

This agreement allowed Missouri to join the Confederacy as a slave state and Maine as a slave state and free and balance slave.

There are no slaves in the Senate Has been maintained?

Indian Removal Act (1830) - President Andrew Jackson enacted policies that forced Native American tribes off their lands to make way for European settlers, resulting in water spots.

Manifest Destiny (1840-1850): This term refers to the belief that the United States has a divine mission to expand the North American continent westward. This belief played a major role in westward expansion, the Oregon Trail, and the Mexican-American War.

Year Civil War (1861-1865) Partisanship and Tension: Deep divisions between Northern and Southern states over slavery, state rights, and economic inequality increased tensions during the Civil War Mid-19th-century United States elections Abraham Lincoln (1860): Lincoln's first Republican Party chairman strongly opposed the expansion of slavery. His election alarmed the Southern states, heightening tensions and eventually leading to secession.

Secession and Confederacy (1860-1861): Eleven southern states seceded from the Union to form the American Confederacy with Jefferson Davis as president.

American Civil War (1861-1865): Approximately 620,000 soldiers were killed in the bloodiest conflict in American history, between the League of Nations (North) and the United States of America (South). Ultimately, it led to the victory of the Confederacy, the abolition of slavery, and the unification of the nation.

The period from the colonial days of the United States to the Civil War covers many of the events, people and ideas that laid the foundation for America today. This brief overview provides insight into the country's complicated history in recent years.

Industrial Revolution and Golden Age:

The Industrial Revolution and Golden Age had a major impact on the American economy, transforming the country from an agrarian society into an industrialized nation.

The Industrial Revolution began in the early 19th century and lasted until the late 1800s.

The Golden Age is a term coined by Mark Twain to refer to the period from the late 1860s to the early 1900s. 1900s. these historical periods are sometimes seen separately but often overlap, both characterized by rapid economic growth and significant social change. During the Industrial Revolution, a number of major inventions and innovations revolutionized the way goods were produced and services were provided.

The main events are as follows. 1. The construction of canals, roads and later railways improved transportation.

2. Invented the cotton pruning machine. Cotton production is rationalized, contributing to the development of the textile industry.
3. The development of the steam engine revolutionized the manufacturing process and enabled the mass production of goods.

4. Form a centralized factory system to increase efficiency and reduce costs.

The golden age after the industrial revolution was marked by rapid economic growth and a move towards monopolies and powerful corporations. The trend of industrialization and urbanization that started earlier continues.

Several major economic developments took place during this period, including:

1. The development of the railway industry not only improved transportation but also stimulated the development of other industries such as steel manufacturing.

2. The rise of powerful corporations and the formation of trusts led to the consolidation of companies and greater control over manufacturing and distribution.

3. Massive waves of immigration to quickly provide cheap labour to developing industries.

4. The expansion of the stock market has encouraged investment in emerging industries. The Industrial Revolution and the Golden Age played an important role in the growth and development of the American economy, but they also had serious drawbacks. These include poor working conditions, economic inequality and environmental degradation. Public interest in these issues contributed to the emergence of the Progressive Era, where laws and reforms started to be made to address these issues.

In short, the Industrial Revolution and the Golden Age were the key factors that shaped the American economy and transformed America into a global industrial powerhouse. These times have brought progress and innovation, as well as social challenges that will shape future generations.

The Great Depression and the New Deal:

The Great Depression and the New Deal were pivotal moments in American economic history.

The Great Depression was a severe economic recession that began in 1929 and lasted about a decade, affecting not only the US economy but also the world market. The New Deal was a series of programs, public works projects, financial reforms, and regulations that President Franklin D. Roosevelt enacted between 1933 and 1939 in response to the Depression.

1. The Great Depression: The stock market crash of 1929 marked the beginning of the Great Depression. By 1933, about 15 million people were unemployed and more than half of the country's banks were broke.

The causes of the Great Depression included poor banking policies, economic imbalances, a lack of regulation, a decline in international trade and massive stock market speculation.

2. The New Deal: In response to the widespread economic hardship of the Great Depression, President Franklin D. Roosevelt introduced the New Deal, which was supposed to provide economic relief and recovery and reform the financial system.

Key elements of the New Deal included:

A. Assistance: To provide immediate assistance to the unemployed and those in financial difficulty, FDR instituted programs such as the Federal Emergency Relief Administration (FERA), which provided grants to states for direct assistance initiatives.

The Civilian Conservation Corps (CCC) provided jobs to unemployed young men to conserve natural resources and preserve public lands.

B. Recovery: Command recovery programs such as the National Industrial Recovery Act (NIRA) and Agricultural Adjustment Act (AAA) were instituted to boost industrial production and farm prices by setting production limits, providing price supports, and regulating labour conditions. Also, the Works Progress Administration (WPA) and the Tennessee Valley Authority (TVA) were formed to create jobs and improve infrastructure.

C. **Reform:** The New Deal introduced financial regulations to prevent future economic crises, such as the Glass-Seagull Act, which separated investment and commercial banks, and the Securities Act of 1933 and the Stock Exchange Act of 1934, which regulated the stock market and called for more transparency. The Social Security Act laid the foundation for America's social safety net, providing benefits for the elderly, disabled, and unemployed. Criticism and Legacy: While the New Deal was responsible for bringing relief and support to millions of Americans, critics argue that it expanded the federal government's role in the economy and did not do enough to end the Great Depression. Others argue that the New Deal did help mitigate the worst effects of the Depression and establish essential social policies that are still in effect today.

Though still controversial, the New Deal remains an integral part of American history and is seen as a precedent for future government intervention in economic crises. - Economic boom after World War II: The post-World War II economic boom, also known as the "Golden Age of Capitalism," was a period of unprecedented economic growth and prosperity in the United States. This boom, which lasted from 1945 into the early 1970s, was characterized by high GDP growth rates, low unemployment, increased consumer demand, and unprecedented technological advances.

Several factors contributed to this period of exceptional growth:

1. The Marshall Plan: This initiative was intended to rebuild European economies after the war and stabilize the region. As a result, Europe required large quantities of American goods, services, and raw materials, which boosted the American economy.

2. Military Spending: The Cold War and the arms race between the US and the Soviet Union resulted in significant spending on research, development, and production of new military technologies, which had a positive impact on the economy in general.

3.   Technological   advances:
Innovations in sectors such as manufacturing, transportation and electronics boosted productivity and economic growth throughout the period. The space race also contributed to rapid technological advances.

4. Keynesian Economic Policies:
The US government instituted Keynesian economic policies that emphasized public spending, full employment, and controlling inflation to promote a stable business climate.

5. Baby Boom: Post World War II population growth resulted in a larger labour force and increased consumer demand, leading to rapid expansion of production and markets.

6. Suburbanization: The mass migration of Americans from the cities to the suburbs led to a construction boom and an increase in automobile production.

7. Expansion of world trade: The establishment of international trade frameworks such as the GATT (General Agreement on Tariffs and Trade) enabled a more open world economic system, leading to increased exports and global economic integration. During this time, the American middle class grew significantly; wages rose and many citizens could enjoy a higher standard of living.

However, the post-WWII economic boom ended in the 1970s due to factors such as the oil crisis, Latin America and increasing global competition.

The role of globalization at the end of the 20th and beginning of the 21st century: Globalization played a significant role in shaping America's economy in the late 20th and early 21st centuries.

This has led to a more connected global market, more competition and trade liberalization.

Key impacts of globalization on the US economy during this period include:

1. Significant growth of national trade: Globalization has accelerated the growth of international trade, which is why cooperation among nations is urgently needed. This has benefited US companies, which have expanded their customer base, sourced cheaper raw materials, and participated more efficiently in global value chains.

2. Contact Us: Globalization has made it easier for people to cross borders, allowing US companies and investors to access foreign markets, investing in companies abroad, and allowing foreign investors to participate in the US economy.

3. Changes in the labour market: outsourcing and offshoring have prevailed in communication in other countries, improvements in communication technology and the free movement of people. This has led to a decline in manufacturing and low-skilled jobs in the US as these functions are relocated to countries with lower labour costs.

At the same time, it has led to an increase in high-skilled jobs in areas such as technology, research and professional services.

4. The Rise of Multinational Corporations (MNCs): As corporations have embraced the opportunities presented by globalization, the power and influence of multinational corporations has increased. US multinationals such as Apple, Google and McDonald's have expanded their global presence, fuelling US economic growth.

5.   Increased   Competition: Globalization has led to increased competition abroad, pushing American companies to improve efficiency and continually innovate to maintain their competitive advantage.

6. Inequality: Globalization has contributed to increasing income inequality in the United States. Job losses due to the outsourcing of low-skilled jobs and increased demand for high-skilled jobs have created a skills shortage that disproportionately affects low-income groups who lack access to education and the resources to adapt.

7. Technology Transfer: Technological advances have spread faster around the world, giving American companies access to innovations that drive productivity and growth. On the contrary: American innovations have contributed to global technological and economic progress. 8th. Cultural spread: The free movement of people, goods and ideas led to increased cultural exchange with other nations in the United States.

This has led to a more diverse society and a greater appreciation for different cultures.

In short, globalization had a profound impact on the US economy in the late 20th and early 21st centuries. While it has created economic growth, access to global markets and technological advances, it has also contributed to job losses, income inequality and increased competition.

CHAPTER 2

The role of capitalism and the free market

- The advantages of capitalism - Free and competitive market

- How capitalism promotes innovation and entrepreneurship

- Economic Movement and the "American Dream"

To introduce in this chapter, we will delve into the impact of capitalism and the free market on society and the economy. Capitalism is the driving force behind unprecedented economic growth, technological advances, and the spread of democracy across the world. We will discuss the virtues of capitalism, the role of the free market and competition, the relationship between capitalism and innovation and the connection between capitalism and the idea of innovation, the concept of the "American dream".

The advantages of capitalism are an economic system based on private ownership of the means of production and distribution of goods and services.

It is built on the principles of voluntary exchange, profit and competition.

One of the major benefits of capitalism is its ability to create wealth through the efficient allocation of resources. By allowing individuals to make their own choices about production, consumption and investment, capitalism fosters entrepreneurship and innovation. Furthermore, a well-functioning capitalist system is often characterized by a high degree of economic freedom.

Businesses and individuals have the freedom to make decisions based on their own preferences and capabilities, which leads to more efficient resource allocation and higher overall productivity.

Free and competitive markets

At the heart of the capitalist system is the concept of the free market, in which firms compete with each other for customers, resources and growth. Competition is the engine of innovation and efficiency, as companies are constantly trying to find new ways to reduce costs and improve their products and services.

To survive and thrive, companies must be able to adapt to changing market conditions and consumer needs. This pressure for change and continuous improvement benefits consumers, who are offered more choice, lower prices, and higher quality goods and services.

How capitalism promotes innovation and entrepreneurship

Innovation and entrepreneurship are undoubtedly two of the most important by-products of capitalism.

Driven by profit motivation and competitive advantage, entrepreneurs and businesses are motivated to find new and better ways to create value for consumers. The market motivates individuals and companies to develop new technologies, approaches and business models to improve efficiency, reduce costs and enhance the consumer experience. In turn, this promotes economic growth and promotes social progress.

Capitalism has been the catalyst for the development of countless innovations, such as computers, smartphones, the Internet and various medical advances. The rewards of success in a competitive marketplace drive entrepreneurs to take risks, invest in research and development, and push the boundaries of what was once thought impossible.

Economic movement and the "American dream" The concept of economic mobility is essential to the capitalist ethos.

It includes the idea that individuals, regardless of their socioeconomic status, have the opportunity to improve their status through hard work, determination and innovation. This is considered the foundation of the "American Dream," a vision that promises prosperity and success to those willing to commit to self-improvement and persevere. The capitalist system has been especially helpful in promoting economic mobility by providing more opportunities for education, investment, and entrepreneurship.

In this system, individuals have the ability to reach their full potential and build a better future for themselves and their families.

In summary, capitalism and the free market play an important role in driving wealth creation, innovation and economic growth around the world. This economic system rewards those who take risks and embrace change, fostering a culture of entrepreneurship and a desire for continuous improvement. Despite its challenges, capitalism remains an essential part of the modern global economy and a major factor in realizing the "American Dream".

CHAPTER 3
INFRASTRUCTURE AND RESOURCES

- America's Vast Natural Resources

- The Historic Importance of Infrastructure Investment

- Transportation Networks, Communication Systems, and Utilities Plus –

Role of Infrastructure in Driving Economic Growth

Introduction

The United States, one of the world's largest and most diverse in the world, is blessed with rich natural resources and extensive infrastructure. These infrastructure networks and resources have played an important role in shaping the growth and development of the nation. In this chapter, we will discuss the United States' natural resources, the historical importance of infrastructure investments, and the complex networks of transportation, communications, and utilities.

Finally, we will explore how these factors contribute to economic growth and the overall quality of life of the country's people.

Vast Natural Resources of the United States

The United States has a multitude of diverse natural resources that are vital to the economic development and prosperity of this nation.

These resources include large amounts of arable land, fertile land, fresh water, minerals, ores, and energy sources such as coal, oil, and natural gas. The country's diverse topographic and climatic conditions also contribute to favourable conditions for the agro-forestry industry.

The abundance of these resources has made the United States one of the world's leading producers of food and energy, but it has also led to the need for responsible management of these resources to ensure sustainability for future generations.

The Historical Importance of Infrastructure Investments

The growth and development of the United States is largely attributable to strategic infrastructure investments made throughout its history. Various government initiatives and policies, such as the construction of the Transcontinental Railroad in the 19th century and the Interstate Highway System in the

20th, have helped connect the territories and the vastness of the country and encouraged economic and commercial expansion. These significant investments have facilitated deeper regional integration, access to essential services and the creation of new industries.

Thus, modern infrastructure in the United States reflects those historic investments and their continued contribution to the country's progress.

Transportation Networks, Communications Systems, and Services

The United States boasts a complex transportation and communications network designed to serve the country's vast territory and population. Transportation networks include roads, highways, railways, airports, seaports, and inland waterways, while communication systems include everything from traditional mail systems and facilities to advanced telecommunications and Internet infrastructure. Utilities, including electricity, natural gas and water supplies, continue to support and drive economic growth and development.

These convenient services ensure that households and businesses have access to essential resources needed for their day-to-day operations and growth.

The role of infrastructure in driving economic growth

Investment in infrastructure is an important component of sustainable economic growth and prosperity.

A robust infrastructure system that promotes trade, encourages regional development and creates employment opportunities is directly related to the construction, maintenance and operation of these systems. Furthermore, reliable transport, communication and utilities networks attract both local and international investors who wish to exploit the accessibility and efficiency offered by these systems. In this way, infrastructure acts as a catalyst for economic growth by stimulating private investment, creating opportunities for innovation and technological advancement, and improving the overall quality of life of people nationwide.

In the United States, vast natural resources and vast infrastructure networks have served as important pillars for the nation's growth and prosperity. Through wise investment and strategic development in transportation, communications, and public services, the country has created a solid foundation on which to build and sustain a diversified economy and continued development. By understanding and appreciating these integral factors, it is becoming increasingly clear how critical infrastructure and resources are in shaping the United States' position as a global leader.

CHAPTER 4

GOVERNMENT INFLUENCE ON ECONOMIC POLICY

- Federal Reserve and monetary policy - Fiscal policy and public spending - Trade policy and international cooperation

 - The importance of stable financial regulation introduction

In today's globalized world, government plays an important role in shaping economic policies in various ways with the aim of achieving economic stability and promoting growth.

In this chapter we will examine how different aspects of government participation, such as Such as the Federal Reserve, fiscal policy, trade policy, and financial regulation can have profound effects on the national and global economy.

I. Federal Reserve and Monetary Policy

The Federal Reserve, also known as the Central Bank of the United States, plays a crucial role in managing the economy through the implementation of monetary policy. This policy refers to the central bank's actions to control the money supply and interest rates.

The Federal Reserve uses several tools to achieve its goals:

1. Open Market Operations - By buying and selling government securities, the Federal Reserve can control the money supply and affect interest rates.

2. Discount Rate - This is the interest rate that the Federal Reserve charges banks for funds they borrow, which can be changed to affect the overall economy.

3. Reserve Requirements: By changing the portion of deposits banks are required to hold as reserves, the Federal Reserve can affect the amount of money available for borrowing and spending. With this monetary policy, the Federal Reserve works to control inflation and maintain stable employment.

II. Fiscal Policy and Public Expenditure

Fiscal policy is the use of government revenue (taxes) and expenditure (spending) to influence the economy. This policy includes:

1. Government Spending: Increasing government spending can boost economic growth by creating jobs and increasing demand for goods and services.

2. Taxation: Changes in tax rates can encourage or discourage certain economic behaviours, which in turn shape the economy. Fiscal policy plays an essential role in stabilizing the economy in times of recession or inflation, implementing expansionary or contractionary measures when necessary. Third Trade policy and international cooperation Trade policy is a set of government policies designed to regulate and promote international trade.

Government influence over trade policy is achieved through:

1. Tariffs: Taxing imported goods can protect domestic industries and generate revenue.

2. Quotas: Setting import volume limits can protect national industries and maintain a balance between local production and international competition.

3. Regulations: Setting safety, labour and environmental standards for goods and services can protect domestic consumers and workers and uphold ethical practices in international trade. International cooperation is crucial for the success of trade policy; this can be achieved through bilateral or multilateral agreements and organizations such as the **World Trade Organization (WTO).**

IV. The importance of stable financial regulation

Financial regulations ensure the stability of the financial sector by creating rules and regulations for financial institutions, markets and instruments. Governments, through regulators, enact these rules to maintain a high level of consumer protection, prevent fraud and promote financial stability.

Key elements of financial regulation include:

1. Capital Requirements: Ensure financial institutions have sufficient capital to cover potential losses.

2. Supervision: Monitoring and enforcing compliance by financial institutions with the rules and thereby controlling systemic risks.

3. Transparency: Promote full and accurate disclosure of information to enable market participants to make effective decisions.

In short, government plays a critical role in shaping economic policy through the Federal Reserve and monetary policy, fiscal policy, trade policy, and maintaining stable financial regulation. Examining and understanding these issues can help provide a comprehensive view of how government is using its influence to promote economic stability, growth and equity.

CHAPTER 5
HUMAN CAPITAL AND TRAINING

- The importance of a skilled workforce - Invest in primary, secondary and university education

- The US university system: incubator for innovation and economic growth

- Immigration and its impact on the workforce To introduce Human capital refers to the knowledge, skills and abilities that individuals possess and bring to the job market. The development of human capital plays an important role in economic growth and prosperity.

In this chapter, we will explore the importance of a skilled workforce, the different levels of investment in education, the unique characteristics of the US university system, and the impact of immigration on the workforce. 5.1 Importance of a skilled workforce A skilled workforce is essential to any thriving economy. Workers with advanced skills, knowledge and capabilities help increase productivity, innovation and competitiveness. A highly skilled workforce capable of adapting to changing technologies and industries, making them invaluable assets in the global economy.

Some of the key benefits include:

1. **Increased productivity:** Skilled workers are more productive and can use resources more efficiently, resulting in lower costs and greater efficiency.

2. **Increased competitiveness:** A skilled workforce fosters innovation, stimulates the development of new industries and enables a country to remain competitive in the global economy.

3. **Economic Development:** As human capital increases, so does economic growth, which leads to higher living standards and reduced poverty rates.

Investments in primary, secondary and tertiary education Investing in primary, secondary and tertiary education is essential for creating a skilled workforce. Education not only equips individuals with skills and knowledge, but also promotes personal development and critical thinking skills necessary for socioeconomic progress. To this end, governments should:

- Develop a comprehensive education policy covering all levels of education

- Allocate adequate resources to ensure that all citizens have access to quality education

- Encourage private sector participation to complement public investment

- Implement targeted interventions to address disparities, such as providing scholarships to disadvantaged groups or promoting STEM fields for female students

The American university system: incubator for innovation and economic growth The US university system is distinguished by its emphasis on flexible, interdisciplinary learning and commitment to research and development. This has made it a hub of innovation and a major engine of economic growth.

Key features include:

- **Public and private funding:** The combination of public and private funding allows for investments in state-of-the-art infrastructure and cutting-edge research.

- **Focus on research:** Universities prioritize research, attracting good faculty and talented students.

- **Partnerships with the private sector:** Universities collaborate with businesses to create hubs for research and knowledge sharing, fostering an ecosystem of innovation and technology transfer.

- **Flexibility:** The system encourages exploration and interdisciplinary learning, enabling students to think critically, innovate and adapt to change.

Immigration and its impact on the workforce

Immigration plays an important role in maintaining a skilled workforce.

By attracting the best talent from around the world, countries can ensure a constant flow of diverse skills, knowledge and expertise.

Here's how immigration contributes to workforce development:

Filling skills shortages: Migrants bring a wide range of skills to the labour market, including important skills in areas such as healthcare, technology and academia.

Encourage innovation: Different streams of ideas, perspectives and cultures foster creative thinking and innovation. Support an aging population: Immigration can help offset the negative effects of an aging workforce by balancing the demographic structure.

A skilled workforce is an integral part of a thriving economy, and investment in primary, secondary and tertiary education is essential for human capital development. The US university system serves as a model for innovation and economic growth, while well-managed immigration policies can provide ongoing access to diverse skills and talents.

CHAPTER 6

American companies: the engine of economic growth

- The power of multinationals - How innovation drives competition and economic growth

- The importance of small and medium-sized enterprises (SMEs)

- Corporate social responsibility and sustainable development

Efforts to introduce American business are the engine of economic growth, drives innovation and competition, and drives job creation in the United States. Multinational corporations, small and medium-sized enterprises (SMEs), and corporate social responsibility organizations have contributed to the booming US economy.

Part 1:

The power of multinational corporations Multinational corporations are an influential force in driving international trade and financial growth. With abundant resources and a global reach, they can navigate complex markets to create innovative products and services, open new markets, and make huge contributions to the global economy.

Their size and presence in many countries allows them to respond quickly to changes in global demand, invest in research and development, and recruit skilled professionals from a variety of backgrounds.

The economic activity generated by these companies has an exponential impact, creating job opportunities throughout the economy, both domestically and internationally.

Part 2:

How innovation drives competition and economic growth Innovation is at the heart of the economic success of American companies.

Companies invest heavily in research and development, identifying new technologies and unique ideas to improve existing products, services and business models. By fostering a culture of constant progress, rooted in a spirit of risk-taking,

companies foster competition in the marketplace. This competitive atmosphere drives companies to continue to grow and innovate, creating better products and services for consumers.

The adoption of digital technology and automation has facilitated greater efficiency, reduced production costs and enabled the rapid introduction of new services. Ultimately, innovation and competition lead to economic growth by expanding markets, creating new jobs and increasing overall productivity.

Part 3:

Importance of Small and Medium Enterprises (SMEs) while multinational corporations often capture the spotlight, small and medium-sized enterprises (SMEs) play an important role in the US economy.

These businesses are often considered the backbone of the country, accounting for a significant percentage of overall employment and productivity. SMBs tend to be flexible, adapt quickly to customer needs and take advantage of niches that larger companies have missed. SMEs also drive economic growth through innovation and job creation.

Many of these businesses began as entrepreneurs who took risks to bring new ideas and products to market. By focusing on agility and flexibility, SMEs contribute to a more diversified economy, thereby strengthening the overall resilience of the economy.

Part 4:

Corporate Social Responsibility and Sustainable Development Efforts In today's increasingly interconnected world, companies must go beyond profit margins and shareholder value; they are also responsible for their environmental and social impact. Corporate social responsibility (CSR) and sustainability have become important issues for businesses of all sizes. Now, both customers and investors are paying more attention to the company's commitment to ethical and environmental practices.

Companies can no longer ignore their social and environmental footprint. By adopting sustainable practices, investing in local communities, and ensuring a diverse and inclusive workplace, companies can drive long-term growth that benefits society.

These efforts not only enhance the company's reputation, but also lay the foundation for a sustainable future for all.

In summary, the economic success of American businesses lies in the synergy of multinational corporations, competition-driven innovation, the vital role of small and medium-sized enterprises, and the growing importance of corporate social responsibility. Together, these forces drive economic growth, create job opportunities, and enhance national prosperity.

CHAPTER 7

Financial Markets and American Prosperity

- The United States is a Global Financial Centre

- The Role of Stock Markets in Economic Growth

- Corporate Lending and Access to Capital

- Risk Creation and Allocation in Derivatives Markets

I will explain the role. Financial markets fuel America's prosperity.

Discover the many factors that make the United States a global financial centre, the role of the stock market in economic growth, the importance of credit and access to capital for financial institutions and small businesses, and the role of the stock market sharing the risk of derivatives.

The United States as a Global Financial Centre

1. Introduction to the United States as a Financial Centre: The Importance of Being at the Centre of Global Financial Activities: New York City and Its Specialized Financial District

2. Large financial institutions

- Role of banks, investment firms and financial services companies

- Key institutions such as the Federal Reserve, IMF, World Bank

3. Financial innovation

- Development of financial products to meet market needs

- Technological advances in the financial sector

II. The role of the stock market in economic growth

1. The stock market is an economic barometer

- It measures economic growth by how the stock market works

- The stock market is a source of capital for companies

2. Resource allocation the stock market is a resource allocation mechanism

- Efficiency is achieved through market decisions

3. Promoting long-term investment

- The role of the stock market in Encouraging investment to foster innovation and growth

- Long-term value creation through capital investment

III. Access to Credit and Capital for Businesses

1. Importance of Credit and Capital for Businesses: Financing Needs for Business Activities, Investments and Expansion Access to Credit is a Key Factor for Business Success

2. Banks and Capital

The Role of Lenders

– Credit and Functions in Credit Markets

– The Importance of government policies and regulations to lending activity

3. Non-bank sources of finance

- Bond markets, venture capital and private equity

- Crowd funding and peer-to-peer lending

IV. Derivatives markets and risk allocation

1. Derivatives market overview

– Definition and purpose of derivatives – Types of derivatives such as options, futures and swap contracts

2. Risk management through derivatives

– Risk mitigation strategies

– Speculation and impact on derivatives markets

3 Regulations

– The importance of regulation to safeguard the Financial Stability

– Lessons from Past Crises

In summary, the United States plays an important role in the global financial system. Domestic financial markets have boosted economic growth and laid the foundation for long-term development and prosperity.

By maintaining a strong financial infrastructure, fostering innovation, and facilitating the efficient allocation of resources, the United States will continue to remain at the centre of global financial activity.

CHAPTER 8

START-UPS AND START ECOSYSTEMS - THE IMPORTANCE OF ENTREPRENEURSHIP FOR ECONOMIC GROWTH

- Start-up Ecosystems: Incubators, Accelerators, and Venture Capital

- Success Stories: From Apple to Tesla, Discover America's Hottest Start-ups

Introduction

The family spirit has long been recognized as a driving force behind violence. We contribute to the realization of economic growth, innovation and job creation. Show your creative qualities, your adaptability and your willingness to take risks to bring your ideas to life. This chapter dives into the world of start-ups, examining the various impacts start-ups have on the economy and examining how start-up ecosystems develop and sustain themselves. Additionally, we will discuss the success stories of well-known American start-ups and how they have transformed the industries in which they operate.

1. The importance of entrepreneurship for economic growth Entrepreneurship is closely linked to economic growth and

prosperity. Entrepreneurs contribute to overall macroeconomic health with their innovative ideas, investment skills and job creation in many ways: - innovating new products and services that increase productivity and boost consumer demand

- disrupting industries and fostering healthy competition

- job opportunities and increase labour productivity

– Contribute to export growth and attract foreign direct investment

2 Start-up ecosystems: incubators, accelerators and venture capital a supportive and inclusive start-up ecosystem is essential to fostering entrepreneurship.

The key components of this ecosystem are incubators, accelerators and venture capital firms:

Incubators: Organizations that provide entrepreneurs with resources to bring their ideas to fruition, including office space, technical support and mentoring. Incubators help early-stage start-ups become self-sufficient businesses.

Accelerator Programs: Programs that accelerate start-up growth through access to capital, mentoring, networking, and workspaces.

We offer a structured program, often focused on a specific industry or technology.

Venture Capital: Financial institutions and individuals invest in start-up companies in exchange for company shares. Venture capital fuels growth by giving companies the resources they need to scale faster and enter new markets.

Success Stories: Discover America's Hottest Start-ups, from Apple to Tesla America has produced some of the most successful and innovative start-ups in the world.

Two good examples are Apple and Tesla, which have revolutionized their industries through continuous innovation and technological advances.

- Apple: Founded in 1976 by Steve Jobs and Steve Wozniak, Apple's mission is to create innovative technologies that can transform the way people experience computers.

Today, Apple is a global giant that makes cutting-edge products like the iPhone, iPad, Mac, and Apple Watch. - Tesla: Founded in 2003 by Elon Musk and a group of engineers, Tesla's goal is to make electric vehicles that are not only environmentally friendly,

But also outperforming conventional vehicles. Since then, Tesla has been at the forefront of electric vehicle innovation, creating vehicles known for their design, performance and technology.

Entrepreneurship plays a key role in boosting the global economy, and ambitious start-ups and innovative ideas will shape the future of industries. By exploring the dynamics of the start-up ecosystem and learning from the successes of Apple and Tesla, we can gain valuable insights into the drivers of growth and continuity in the start-up scene.

CHAPTER 9
THE FUTURE OF THE US ECONOMY

- The challenges facing the US economy: income inequality, outdated infrastructure and growing national debt
- Impact of technology and automation on the labour market - The role of sustainable energy and green industry in future growth Strategies to ensure continued prosperity. To introduce the future of the American economy is undeniably crucial to the nation's progress and stability.

With humorous challenges ahead, this chapter examines the key aspects that will shape the economic landscape, tackling income inequality, aging infrastructure and the growing national debt, and analyzes the impact of new technologies and the role of sustainable energy.

1. Challenges for the US economy

A. Income inequality

In recent decades, the gap between rich and poor has widened in the United States. This growing income inequality has a number of negative effects on the economy, including stagnating social mobility, reduced economic growth and increased dependency on care. In the future, education-focused policies, progressive taxation, minimum wage reform, and workplace equality can help alleviate these challenges.

B. outdated infrastructure

America's infrastructure has been in trouble for several years and is increasingly becoming an economic burden. To meet this challenge, significant investments are needed, especially in transport, water systems and energy infrastructure, which can create new jobs, stimulate trade and improve the economic performance of the wider economy.

C. Increase in the national debt

The US national debt has surpassed $28 trillion and continues to grow, raising concerns about fiscal responsibility and long-term economic stability. It is imperative for the government to balance spending cuts with income growth, implement responsible fiscal policies and ensure long-term economic growth.

2. Impact of technology and automation on the labour market

Technological advancement and increased automation have led to significant changes in the labour market. While these changes have created new opportunities and increased efficiency, they have also resulted in job displacements and the need to upskill.

Government agencies and businesses must work together to provide access to education, training and retraining initiatives, ensuring the workforce is prepared for the job ahead.

3. The role of sustainable energy and green industries in future growth.

The transition to sustainable energy and green industries presents a significant opportunity for the US economy. Embracing renewable energy sources, promoting green jobs and investing in environmentally friendly technologies will not only ensure a cleaner and healthier environment, but will also promote economic growth and sustainable global competitiveness.

4. Strategies to ensure continued prosperity

To ensure continued prosperity, the US economy needs to focus on several key strategies:

A.   Promote   innovation Technological progress and innovation should always be at the forefront of the American economic agenda. Investments in education, research and development, and support for disruptive start-ups will prove important in developing a strong economy of the future.

B. Educational priority

Education reform must remain a top priority. By focusing on developing a skilled workforce with a strong STEM background, the United States can maintain its competitive edge in the global marketplace.

C. Infrastructure reconstruction

A comprehensive, long-term plan must be adopted to upgrade and maintain the nation's infrastructure, thereby creating jobs, securing future economic growth opportunities, and ensuring the resilience of the US supply chain.

4. Global trade and cooperation

The United States must remain committed to global trade and cooperation, take advantage of international markets, and address related challenges. Engaging with global partners will foster prosperity and facilitate the sharing of resources, ideas and expertise. The future of the US economy depends on that country's ability to address the related challenges discussed in this chapter. Addressing income inequality, investing in infrastructure, managing the national debt, embracing new technologies and prioritizing sustainable energy will be key to shaping a thriving US economy in the coming years.

The secret to America's strong economy lies not in any single factor, but in a combination of historical, geographic, political, and cultural factors that have fostered an environment conducive to growth and improvement. As we navigate the ever-changing global economic landscape, we must continue to learn from the United States' experience and adapt these strategies to the unique challenges and opportunities ahead.

CONCLUSION

Unravelling the foundations of prosperity involves understanding the key factors that contribute to creating and maintaining a thriving economy, both for individuals and for society at large.

Here are the essential factors that contribute to prosperity:

1. Rule of law: A stable legal system based on the objective, fair and transparent application of the law is essential to attract investment, promote entrepreneurship and ensure a level playing field.

2. Ownership: The ability to own, transfer and protect assets, including intellectual property, is critical to encouraging innovation and driving economic growth.

3. Sound Currency: A stable, non-manipulated currency is necessary for a thriving economy. It helps control inflation, promotes long-term investment and ensures people maintain confidence in the value of their money.

4. Free Market: Open and competitive markets lead to efficient allocation of resources as well as the discovery of new products and services.

It also includes minimizing government intervention, unless necessary to protect consumers or maintain a competitive environment.

5. Human capital: a skilled and well-educated population is more productive and creative, directly contributing to economic growth. Investments in education and capacity-building programs are essential for human resource development.

6. Trade: Both international and domestic trade help promote economic growth by allowing countries to specialize in goods and services for which they have a comparative advantage. This stimulates innovation, productivity and cross-border consumption.

7. Social Capital: Trust, cooperation and communication in society are essential for the smooth functioning of the economy. It reduces transaction costs and helps maintain an environment conducive to manufacturing efforts.

8. Infrastructure: Reliable infrastructure, including transportation, communications, and utilities, is critical to the efficient functioning of the economy, connecting people, goods, and services, thereby stimulating both trade and productivity.

9. Governance and institutions: Effective and efficient governance systems, with the institutions that underpin them, are key to attracting investment, building trust, ensuring the rule of law and enabling the market economy to function well.

10. Innovation and Entrepreneurship:

Fostering an environment that encourages innovation and entrepreneurship is important in the long run, as it leads to more competitive industries, job creation and faster economic growth.

Unravelling the foundations of prosperity requires an integrated and comprehensive understanding of these factors which, when combined, will pave the way for sustainable economic growth and improved well-being for societies.